Serenity

Church Library

This book
presented by

Dr. & Mrs. Charles Newman

to

The Lamppost Library
Christ United Methodist Church

In Honor of

Mr. & Mrs. Clifford Marmann

By the Same Author

Splendor from the Sea
As a Tree Grows
Bold under God—A Fond Look at a Frontier Preacher
A Shepherd Looks at Psalm 23
A Layman Looks at the Lord's Prayer
Rabboni—Which Is to Say, Master
A Shepherd Looks at the Good Shepherd and His Sheep
A Gardener Looks at the Fruits of the Spirit
Mighty Man of Valor—Gideon
Mountain Splendor
Taming Tension
Expendable
Still Waters
A Child Looks at Psalm 23
Ocean Glory
Walking with God
On Wilderness Trails
Elijah—Prophet of Power
Salt for Society
A Layman Looks at the Lamb of God
Lessons from a Sheep Dog
Wonder o' the Wind
Joshua—Man of Fearless Faith
A Layman Looks at the Love of God
Sea Edge
David I
David II
Sky Edge
Chosen Vessels
In the Master's Hands
Predators in Our Pulpits
Songs of My Soul
Thank You, Father
God Is My Delight

Serenity

Finding God Again for the First Time

W. Phillip Keller

BAKER BOOK HOUSE
Grand Rapids, Michigan 49516

Contents

Preface

here are men and women who may have succeeded well in every realm of living except their spirits. They may have attained wealth, power, prestige, and popularity, yet be poor in spirit. It is significant of the twentieth century that despite our increased affluence, greater leisure, and longer life with all of its technological advances, mankind is more restless and dissatisfied than ever before. Regardless of all that money, science, research, and sociological studies can do, the inner heart hungers for more than just materialistic answers to the questioning spirit.

This inner longing, this quest for purpose to living, is one of the greatest tensions of our times. Yet there is really nothing new about this inner restlessness of the human heart. From earliest times it has been with men.

Augustine, the ancient seer of North Africa, put it in a nutshell when he wrote: "Oh God, thou hast made us for thyself, and our hearts are restless, searching till they find their rest in thee."

That the search goes on cannot be denied. Everywhere men seek solace for the tension within. They turn to every conceivable sort of teaching, philosophy, religion, or mysticism for meaning to living.

I

Knowing God

any, like derelict ships adrift, are swept hither and yon on the changing tides of thought and learning. There is no direction to their course. They sense this lack of direction and they fear the future.

So it is proper for us to ask these simple questions. "Is it really possible to find inner peace and tranquility? Is there something or someone that can help us tame these inner tensions? Is there a rest to be found for our restless, questioning spirits?"

The answer to each query is yes! As Augustine put it so precisely, "Our hearts are restless, searching till they find their rest in thee."

It is possible to find God. It is, moreover, possible to really know him in a personal and intimate manner. By this I am not implying that one finds religion, or knows *about* God. What I am saying is much more direct than that. I am saying it is perfectly possible to enter into a personal, firsthand acquaintance with God. Then once we have met him, it is possible to have this introduction grow into a very deep and enduring friendship. But beyond even this there is the sublime sense in which we come to feel a part of the family of God: He is in fact a Father to us and we are his contented children. And it is in this context that great serenity sweeps over our lives. We know where we belong at last. We have come home. The wandering is over. The search is ended. The soul is at rest.

The difficulty is that a lot of very sincere people do not believe this is possible. They claim it is self-delusion. Like Karl Marx they insist it is like an opiate with which one can be drugged. But the truth is just the opposite. To those who have found God and know him, he is the most meaningful person in life. He alone brings order and purpose out of what otherwise would be chaos and confusion.

Whether we wish to admit it or not, we live amid a confusion of thought. This chaos creates enormous turmoil in our times and brings in its train a whole host of tensions and anxieties. Therefore it must follow that if we can find and come to know one who is able to give clear direction to us in our dilemma, the anxieties will evaporate. We will know where we are going and in that knowledge and assurance we shall find peace of heart and quietness of mind.

How, then, do we get to know God? How do we find him? How can we make contact? Where do we go to get an introduction?

Strange to say, and this may startle many readers, he is and has been even more anxious to meet us. He has gone to great lengths to insure that we can get to know him.

He has chosen to show himself to us in four ways. We must recognize, of course, that God is no mere person. It is true he has personality, he has character, he is capable even of assuming our humanity, but he is not a mere human being. He is also infinite in all of his attributes. Because of this, though able to identify with us, he is far beyond us and therefore deserving of our deepest respect and devotion.

He has deigned to reveal himself to us in rather simple yet effective ways. They are simple enough that an untutored savage or even a small child can understand. Yet they are effective enough to elicit a response from the most brilliant mind and highly developed intellect, provided that intellect is not blinded and bigoted by its own pride and self-importance.

Here are the four ways to knowing God.

First of all he has given to us a concept of his character in the natural and created universe which he brought into being. The beauty and brilliance of flowers, trees, birds, skies, clouds, grass, hills, mountains, streams, sun, moon, stars, and ten thousand other forms of animals, insects, plants, and fishes are utterly beyond the mind of man to explain. It is not enough to say they are the product of physical and biological forces working by blind impulse or mere whimsy. The order, unity, and obvious thoughtful design that run through every segment of the universe speak eloquently of a master mind and indulgent creator. There is nothing casual or random about it. It all functions with meticulous precision and meaningful progress. It all denotes careful planning with a specific purpose in mind.

All that is noble and fine in our own human cultures and society must make us pause and wonder about the natural world. Our own responses to the song of a bird, the graceful motion of a swan, the glory of a sunrise or sunset, are more profound than the mere interaction of chemicals or reaction of our bodies to physical stimuli.

Something within our own spirits answers to the divine spirit in quiet assurance that all of this beauty and design and order are a part of his character and mind. To repudiate them is to ignore God. To deliberately shut our souls to this self-disclosure by God is to refuse to accept his overtures to us.

Paul, the great thinker and mighty intellect of the early Christian era, put it this way in rather blunt but unmistakable language:

> Since the beginning of the world the invisible attributes of God, for example, his eternal power and divinity, have been plainly discernible through things which he has made and which are commonly seen and known, thus leaving these men without a rag of excuse. They knew all the time that there is a God, yet they refused to acknowledge him as such, or to thank him for what he is or does. Thus they became fatuous in their argumentations, and plunged their silly minds still further into the dark. (Rom. 1:20–21 [PHILLIPS])

The very reason why many people today find it impossible to attain peace of heart is that they deliberately refuse to admit that God even exists. We must face the fact that it takes two people to have friendship. It takes two people to establish a father-child relationship. And if one of the parties persists in deliberately denying that the other one exists, not even acknowledging that he is alive, how can one possibly hope for a meeting? How can there be any contact? How can any acquaintance even begin?

I am aware that, especially for the intellectually sophisticated person, it requires pocketing one's pride to look for God in the natural world. But he is there, waiting quietly and patiently to meet the open heart and open mind. And when he does, he always brings peace.

Secondly, we can know God through the lives and personalities of other people. Almost all of us at some time or another in life have encountered individuals who are entirely different from other people. There is a unique spirit of goodwill, wholesomeness, and warmhearted generosity about them. Very often we are surprised to discover that they have not always been like this, that at some point in their past there has been a direct encounter between them and God. He has entered into their lives in a most intimate manner. The result was a complete change of conduct and alteration of attitudes.

There is something intensely attractive about the spirit of these people. They are serene, tranquil, and joyous in a dimension that does us great good. It is a pleasure to be with them and sense the love and character of God in their lives.

I clearly recall the first stranger of this sort I ever met. I had been sent 250 miles away from home at the age of eight to attend a boarding school. Naturally I felt torn up about it. The big, rambling, barnlike building where we were housed and taught seemed a gloomy, dark, cold, forbidding place. Most of the staff struck me as being a stiff crowd of rather cruel characters. Certainly their conduct did little for a small lad, far from home and quite frightened by this grim and austere world.

Only the principal was a different sort of person. She was a tiny, misshapen, homely little lady who had ever known good health. Her back was hunched, her arms and legs were scrawny, her face was plain, her straight hair was pulled back in a tight bun.

But we boys and girls scarcely saw these characteristics at all. Instead there radiated from within this little bundle of humanity so much love, so much warmth, so much downright goodness, so much sweet serenity and contentment that we were drawn towards her in a dramatic way. So much did we love this woman that we boys would actually fight each other just for the favor of carrying home her briefcase of books. Some of us have corresponded with her continuously for over forty years. Her life is still speaking for God.

Her secret was simple. She knew God. She loved him. She walked and talked with him. She reflected his character to us children. And many of us came to know him because we first saw what he was really like through her life.

The third way in which it is possible to know God is through his own self-revelation in writing. A great deal has been written down through the long history of mankind to help us know God. From earliest times those men and women who had intimate contacts with him attempted to express their insights by both the spoken and written language of their race.

There has, of course, been a certain degree of controversy as to how much of what was written was inspired. Yet the fact remains that sufficient has been put into human language to help any truly seeking heart to find and know God.

The greatest single compilation of divine revelation is contained within the small library of sixty-six books, written by some forty different authors over a period of 1,500 years, commonly called *the Scriptures* or *the Bible*. No other single source of written material has enabled so many men and women to know God. It has been read by millions of people in hundreds of languages all over the earth.

In addition to this collection of writings, which we accept as being inspired by the Spirit of God because of their unity, authenticity, and ability to change human lives, there is a great mass of other helpful material. There are sacred hymns, songs, and psalms. There are great sermons. There are devotional meditations. There are spiritual discourses by devout and godly thinkers. There are tracts, pamphlets, and numerous other regular publications to help people to *know God.*

Of course, studying the Scriptures themselves is the surest way to knowing God. It entails time, meditation, thought, prayer, and an open spirit that is not prejudiced with personal pride. The number of people who have learned to love God and know him well in this way runs into many, many millions. This is especially true today when new translations in modern idiom make reading the Bible so much more relevant.

I am prepared to say that anyone disturbed in spirit can find ease of heart and mind in this book. Only one condition is required. The reader must come in humility, prepared to make the moral commitments and decisions which a diligent study will demand. Begin with the Gospel of John. It could well be the key to unlocking a whole new world of quiet joy and serene contentment for your spirit.

Finally, the fourth way in which we can know God is through the life and person of Jesus Christ. Most of our information about his life is contained in the New Testament, though other books concerning his teachings abound.

If I may be pardoned for saying so, there are really three Jesus Christs. I put it this way to be as plain and helpful as I can. But before I explain, may I make it abundantly clear that this person was not just a man. He was in absolute fact God in human form. He was the "God-man"—Jesus—the Christ.

There is first the historical Jesus Christ. He is best known to most people as a Jewish teacher who lived roughly twenty centuries ago in Palestine. He was accused of blasphemy by the ecclesiastical hierarchy and finally committed to crucifixion by the ruling Romans. To know this much about him is not to know him or to know God.

Secondly, there is the theological Jesus Christ. He is perhaps more obscure than the historical Jesus. He is held tenuously in the thinking of many great scholars, teachers, and even laymen as the propounder of profound truth. It is perfectly possible to be steeped in all of his teachings, to be able to dissect and debate his discourses, yet not really know him or God.

Thirdly, there is the actual, living, Lord Jesus Christ. Though he once lived among us as a man, he is in fact God.

His teachings were divine. His death was his own deliberate redemptive act on our behalf and in our stead. His bodily resurrection was positive evidence of his power over both death and decay. It is he who shattered for all time the shackles of both sin and death that bind the human heart. By his living Spirit he comes even now to reside within our spirits if we invite him. It is he who sets us free from our anxieties and tensions. To know this Christ is to know God.

2

Faith: What It Is and How It Works

p to this point in the book a very deliberate effort has been made to discuss the subjects under consideration in a logical manner. No effort has been spared to appeal to the reason of the reader so that he may understand what forces produce tension either in the body or mind and how to counteract those influences.

But when we moved into the less well known and less familiar area of the human spirit in the preceding chapter, no doubt certain difficulties began to arise for some. The reader may have begun to feel a bit lost.

This is easy to understand. Most of us from our childhood have been conditioned to think in terms of only visible or tangible things. These we generally refer to as being "real."

Somehow most of us are very much more at ease discussing or dealing with such solid subjects as our homes, family, friends, money, food, or clothing. A few people are bold enough to try to talk about abstract things like hope, love, joy, and peace, if they are pushed into it. But as a rule the majority shy away from such subjects simply because it seems in no time they are a bit beyond their depth. Even though love, joy, faith, and sincerity may play important roles in their lives, they do not discuss them except on rare occasions and then only in confidence with a close friend.

When we move out beyond this realm to the region of our relationship to God, who is Spirit, we almost always find people are even more unsure of themselves. In a peculiar way they become almost paralyzed. It is as if spiritual matters are quite beyond them. They act as if this were an area of discussion entirely out of this world.

In a way this is exactly so. It is not that matters of the spirit are of no consequence in life. Quite the opposite—they are of paramount importance. Rather, the difficulty is in trying to use our logic and reason to grasp ideas which are essentially of the spirit and beyond the bounds of mere human intellect.

Paul, perhaps the greatest intellect of his time, explains this very clearly in his first letter to the young church at Corinth:

> God has, through the Spirit, let us share his Secret. For nothing is hidden from the Spirit, not even the deep wisdom of God. For who could really understand a man's inmost thoughts except the spirit of the man himself? How much less could anyone understand the thoughts of God except the very Spirit of God? And the marvelous thing is this, that we now receive not the spirit of the world but the Spirit of God himself, so that we can actually understand something of God's generosity toward us.
>
> It is these things that we talk about, not using the expressions of the human intellect but those which the Holy Spirit teaches us, explaining spiritual things to those who are spiritual.

But the unspiritual man simply cannot accept the matters which the Spirit deals with—they just don't make sense to him, for, after all, you must be spiritual to see spiritual things. The spiritual man, on the other hand, has an insight into the meaning of everything, though his insight may baffle the man of the world. This is because the former is sharing in God's wisdom. . . . Incredible as it may sound, we who are spiritual have the very thoughts of Christ. (1 Cor. 2:10–16 [PHILLIPS])

In light of this I believe it is fair and appropriate to say that in order to grasp spiritual facts we must pass beyond the realm of logic and reason to that of faith. Of course at this point many sincere people will insist that human intelligence is sufficient to untangle the tightest knots of life. They will declare vehemently that anything outside the frame of reference of human logic is pure wishful thinking. They will want to dismiss the entire spiritual realm with a casual shrug because it is not subject to the basic scientific approach of observable phenomena.

I admit quite freely and frankly that for such people there really is very little use in reading on any further in this book. If they are being absolutely sincere and utterly honest in their contentions that no spiritual realm exists, or that if it does, it is most definitely on the periphery of life and not at its center, then what follows simply will not make sense.

But if the reader, at any time, has experienced even the tiniest hint of an inner longing, a peculiar pull toward a higher power than himself or herself, a strange bittersweet tension of wanting to be somewhat better, then the balance of this book may well ease that tension.

First of all, may I repeat at the outset that it demands a certain degree of intellectual fortitude from most of us to admit we need someone or something bigger than ourselves in life. We are generally so fully preoccupied with *I* and *me* as being the most important person in all the world that we cannot conceive of anyone else usurping this position in our life. Unfortunately it is not until the stresses and storms of life have just about wrecked us that we decide to turn elsewhere for help or tranquility.

Many people assume that there is no God, or that if there is one, he is so remote and far removed from life that he simply does not count. Others have a rather detached view of him as a benevolent being who occasionally enters their affairs. They hope that by an occasional visit to a church he will be placated to the point where perhaps he will do them a good turn if they get in a tight spot.

For all such people the things of the Spirit are on the very perimeter of life. They are relatively unimportant. They can be taken or left at will. They have virtually no bearing whatever on personal behavior. People who think this way have attempted to reduce spiritual concepts to the common ground of reason. They look on all spiritual values and relationships very lightly. Because of this they never dream that those same spiritual ideas might well prove to hold the very inner secret to life itself.

It takes some real courage to pocket our intellectual pride, face ourselves for what we are, and admit honestly that we need someone greater than ourselves to move into our lives and manage our affairs. It takes even greater courage to admit to ourselves that we need to be made over from the inside out.

I am not here writing about just theoretical or theological hypotheses. From grievous, personal, firsthand experience I know what agony of soul and anguish of heart are the lot of a man or woman far from God. Or, put in a different way, I have known the emptiness, the frustration, the pointlessness of a life which outwardly may have appeared successful but inwardly was empty and meaningless. I know the tension of trying to live my own life in my own way, while keeping God at arm's length only as a nodding acquaintance.

By the time I was into my early forties I had achieved every ambition I ever set myself in life. I had a beautiful wife, lovely children, a fine home, an excellent income, many friends, an international reputation in several fields, and a memory packed full of adventures from around the world. But inside I was hollow and empty and unfulfilled. I knew I was not the man I ought to be and I ached with a deep inner ache for something better.

Oh, I knew all about Christianity. I knew all about the church. I knew all about the historical Jesus. I was even fairly well acquainted with the theological Jesus. But I really and truly did not know God. He was not real. He was not alive. He was not active in my affairs. He was not at the center of my considerations or my deliberations. He did not control my conduct. He was not important to me. Deep down inside I wanted him to be, but I did not know how to accomplish this. It was like being hungry and thirsty yet finding no way to satisfy that hunger or appease that awful thirst. How could I tame this inner tension?

Then one day I read a very simple statement from Jesus' famous and well-known Sermon on the Mount. In it he said unequivocally, "Blessed are they which do hunger and thirst after righteousness: for they shall be filled" (Matt. 5:6).

This was a categorical statement. There were no special conditions attached to it. There were no strings to it. It was not a question of reason, or logic, or thought. It was simply a straightforward case of accepting what had been said. And that is just what I did. There was nothing more involved than my complete inner accord.

It was as if I reiterated silently, "Oh God, you have declared through your Son, Jesus Christ, that if I hunger and thirst after righteousness I shall be filled. Here I am, expecting it to happen."

And it did.

God did just that. He came. His Spirit penetrated my spirit. There was a simple, quiet, serene awareness that the living Christ had come into my life by his Spirit.

There was no emotional upheaval. There was no disquieting disturbance. It was an encounter between my spirit and the Spirit of God himself. I was standing alone at the time on a high cliff overlooking a river that wound out across the plains from the Rockies. In a sense it was as though the Spirit of God coming from the very heart of God flowed into my being in the same way that the river at my feet flowed into the empty valley before me from the snow-mantled mountains.

How had it happened?

By faith.

Faith is beyond reason. It is outside logic. It is the response of a man's spirit to the Spirit and person of God.

The greatest obstacle to the functioning of faith is intellectual pride. Its greatest incentive is humility.

Now, as I have said earlier in the book, no one is either very keen or really able to humble himself. But circumstances and events in life have a way of humbling most of us at one time or other. And when they do we can be deeply grateful if they turn us to God.

But over and beyond all of this I do believe that reason and logic can help us to prepare our own inner hearts for faith. Surely most of us can see that life is far too complex and the world we live in too complicated for us to cope with all its difficulties alone. There is, if we are really honest about it, a need we sense to have someone greater than ourselves to whom we can turn for courage and wisdom beyond our own ability.

Just admitting this to be the case can set the proper stage for spiritual awareness. The Scriptures are very clear in emphasizing that God is pleased to enter a humble human heart by his Spirit. He actually delights to do this. But by the same measure the Scriptures are likewise very emphatic in pointing out that God actually resists and rejects those who are proud and haughty.

When in humility we approach him in faith, it is amazing how he responds. He loves to meet us. Our faith in him delights him no end. We are actually told, "Without faith it is impossible to please [God]" (Heb. 11:6).

It is by faith that we know God exits. It is by faith that we sense the presence of his Spirit in communication with our spirits. It is by faith that we become acquainted with the living person Jesus Christ. It is by faith that we invite him to enter our lives as a friend, a savior, and eventually as our manager.

In all of this there is a gradual but nonetheless very real shift of interest in our affairs from a self-centered *I* or *me* to another—*he*—the living God. And as this relationship ripens we find it maturing into seeing ourselves no longer as solitary souls but as members of a family, the family of God.

This is part of the fascinating and wondrous work done by the Spirit of God himself within my spirit. It is he who makes me keenly aware that I have become a child of God. It is he who makes me feel very much accepted by God as my Father. It is he who brings home to me again and again the calm, quiet assurance that because I am his child and he is my Father, all of my activities, welfare, and life are very much his immediate concern.

Within such a real and vital personal relationship many of the problems and the complexities in life lose their fear. There is a sense of reassuring security which enfolds me, and I become a relaxed and serene sort of person. "God hath not given us the spirit of fear; but of power, and of love, and of a sound mind" (2 Tim. 1:7).

To live in this atmosphere, with this attitude of mind, is not to have found an escape hatch through which one ducks to avoid the harsh realities of living. Quite the contrary. It is to face positively all the futilities and frustrations and fears with a calm, quiet spirit free of tension and undue anxiety.

Better still, this firsthand acquaintance between a person and the living God adds great significance and special meaning to all one's movements. There is a new awareness that life is much more than just a haphazard sequence of random events. There is a growing consciousness that even the trivial details do have import and consequence, not only for me as a child of God, but also for all others whom my life and influence touch.

I know of nothing else in all the world which gives such tremendous dignity to living. I know of nothing else which so constrains me to live life on a level above the common crowd. I know of nothing else which infuses such an aura of adventure and excitement into living as the concept that God my Father cares very deeply what I do and how I do it. This idea lifts me from the level of living as I like—just any old way—to living with great purpose and enormous depth.

In this discussion I am deliberately avoiding the scriptural or theological language used in the Bible to portray this pattern of life. But to give the reader an inkling of how far Scripture goes in this direction, I would point out that there are passages which refer to God's children as "ambassadors," as "priests," as "heirs" of God and "joint heirs with Christ," even as "kings."

Now all of this is both possible and practical through faith, this faith having as its object God himself, and his own declarations of commitment to us. It is true to say he does not ask us to to do anything more than he himself is prepared to match. He does not invite us to commit ourselves to him without in turn committing himself to us. Knowing God in an intimate way is very much a two-way proposition. The instant we respond by faith in any way either to him or his statements, he reciprocates. The net result is a most cordial cooperative relationship.

Put in another way, God himself is faithful to himself; he is faithful to his commitments; he is faithful to his friends; he is faithful to his children. The person who makes this firsthand discovery moves into a marvelous area of carefree living. This is perhaps the most important statement made in this entire book. There is absolutely nothing else which can guarantee quiet repose and happy confidence in life—only the personal, firsthand knowledge that comes from experiencing the faithfulness of God.

All through our careers we may have found other human beings unreliable. We may have felt people were fickle and unpredictable. We may have been let down, double-crossed, misunderstood, and even hated without cause. All of life, its events and its supposed realities, may have mocked us. We may have feared to put reliance on anything or anyone. But anyone who has really and truly had a firsthand encounter with God will know from experience that he is utterly reliable, unchanging, and ever faithful.

No doubt there will be some who read this and say, "Oh, that's all very well for those who have faith, but what about the rest of us who haven't got this faith? How does one get it? Or if one has a wee bit how can it be increased or strengthened?"

There are several fairly simple answers to these questions.

First of all it needs to be understood that everyone has a chance to demonstrate or exercise faith. For faith is actually an act of my will in response to God. If I react or respond positively when he comes to me, there is cooperation on my part. This is positive faith or, as Scripture calls it, "the faith of obedience."

If, on the other hand, I react negatively, I reject his overtures deliberately. I refuse to cooperate; I will not believe in what I have seen, heard, or know of God—no matter how he tries to make contact with me.

It will be recalled that in the previous chapter I said God could be known through nature, through other people's godly lives, through what had been written or spoken of him, and through his Son Christ Jesus.

The Spirit of God may use any one of these four ways to approach us. If we spurn and reject his approach, of course he can do no more. It takes two to make a mutual contact. He may come again and again, but my refusal to respond demonstrates not only the deliberate exercise of my will but also lack of faith.

If, on the other hand, an individual does react positively, if there is a cooperative response, this is faith in action, otherwise known as the faith of obedience, which is such a thrill to God.

Assuming now that one has exercised even just a faint glimmer of faith, how can it be increased? The most simple way is to be humble enough to acknowledge openly we have little faith and ask God pointblank to give us the fortitude to act in faith. The cry of the distressed soul who came to Christ and pleaded, "Lord, I believe, help thou mine unbelief!" is a classic example of honesty which was immediately honored and vindicated.

We are given to understand clearly that faith is one of the gifts which God's Spirit enjoys bringing to hungry hearts. So if there is an obvious lack of simple faith, just ask for it. He will be delighted to grant the request.

There are a few commonly held misunderstandings about faith. There is the idea abroad that the success or failure of one's acquaintance with and confidence in God depends on the degree of faith one has. It is wrongly assumed that if there is great, strong faith, fantastic results will occur. If faith is weak, then little will happen. Jesus in his comparison of faith to a grain of mustard seed held this whole concept up to ridicule.

The important thing to remember about faith is that it is the object upon which it is centered that validates it, not the inherent strength or weakness of the faith itself. If faith, no matter how weak, responds to and resides in God and in his Son Christ Jesus, it becomes strong, virile, unshakable. If, on the other hand, our faith, even though enormous, is centered in circumstances or changing human nature, then it is likely to be broken, crushed, and rendered of no avail simply because it is lodged in something unreliable.

Perhaps a simple illustration will help the reader to grasp this cardinal concept. I hope ardently it may also encourage someone to put his confidence in God.

Let us suppose a young lady falls in love with a handsome young man who appears to have excellent qualities. She responds to his advances. She has enormous faith in him. She accepts his proposal. They are married and so enter a mutual life of commitment. In due course he proves to be unfaithful. Her heart is shattered. Her home is broken. Her dreams are dashed. It is doubtful indeed if ever again she can have a particle of faith in any man.

But by and by she meets another gentleman. Again something about his approach attracts her. She has to muster all her resources to trust him. Her faith in him is very feeble, very flickering. Finally she decides to give marriage another try. But she is not at all sure. Her man this time turns out to be utterly reliable. She has a happy heart. Her home is a joy. Her fondest dreams are fulfilled.

What has made the difference? Is it her great faith or little faith? Neither. The degree of her faith had nothing to do with it.

The difference was made by the caliber of the person in whom her faith resided. It was the character of the second man that made her faith a glorious joy.

And so it is with our faith in God. It does not depend on either its own inherent strength or its weakness. It depends, rather, entirely on the character and person of God himself.

Because God is who he is and has such an impeccable character we may be utterly sure our confidence in him, our faith in him, will never be betrayed. What a tonic for tension!

3

The Character of Christ

I t was Jesus Christ himself who made the unequivocal statement, "He that hath seen me hath seen the Father" (John 14:9). All through his years of public appeal and teaching Jesus repeatedly emphasized this point. He made it abundantly clear that he and his Father were one, that he was doing exactly what his Father would do, that he so lived in God and God his Father so lived in him that they were in fact one and the same person.

This, then, being the case, it is obvious that to understand and appreciate the character of God, we must of necessity look at the character of Christ. To see the one is to see the other.

One of the gigantic achievements accomplished during the few short years of Christ's life was the precise portrayal given to us of God himself. Sometimes I feel we miss this point completely. Paul makes much of it. He declares dramatically in

Colossians 1:15, "Now Christ is the visible expression of the invisible God" (PHILLIPS).

In view of the above facts we should not hesitate, then, to take a long, hard look at the life of our Lord. He is the one in whom we are putting our confidence. He is the one who must of necessity validate our faith. He is the one who ultimately vindicates the reliance invested in him. He is the one who makes our relationship in a spiritual dimension both real and workable. He is the one who makes genuine Christianity a superior and serene way of life.

In essence it is Christ himself who makes our Christian faith unique among the world's many religions, creeds, philosophies, and teachings. Jesus, the Christ, was not a mere man; he was not just another "good" man; he was not just another prophet in the long succession of prophets; he was not just a moralizer with a higher code of ethics; he was not just another great thinker; he was not just a mighty philosopher of unusual perception; he was not just a new teacher of radical or revolutionary ideals.

The truth is that he was all of these and much more. He was God in human guise. He was God garbed in human flesh, expressing himself through human personality. In so doing he gave us a precise portrayal of God's character. In the very nature of things he could not do otherwise. He had to be true to himself, and he was.

This brings us to first concept of his character that arouses our attention and admiration. He was not only utterly truthful but he was truth. This is a formidable fact for us to face.

The vast majority of our problems in human relations stem from the simple fact that people are not true. People from childhood are drilled in duplicity. It is not that they deliberately set out to be scoundrels, but rather that they tend to twist, distort, and manipulate matters in such a way as to always protect themselves. All of us are caught up in the vicious struggle of self-preservation. Therefore something must be sacrificed to insure our survival, and more often than not it is truth which is made the victim.

Basically this explains our human sense of insecurity. Again and again through life we hear the common comment, "I just cannot trust him!" This lack of trust that is so apparent between people lies at the heart of much human tension. The fact that we find even friends unreliable tends to fill us with apprehension. Men and women discover through the most bitter and burning experiences that even members of their own families may prove false. They simply are not true to one another. Or, put another way, there is no truth in their statements nor in their behavior.

I am keenly aware that some still contend that the majority of human beings are basically honest. This contention simply is not so. If it were, there would be no need for laws or codes of human conduct to control society.

The enormous lengths taken in almost every area of life for self-protection stand as undeniable evidence that we human beings really don't trust each other. We put confidence in one another only to the degree that our self-interests are safeguarded and preserved by all sorts of complex social rules and regulations. These are laid down in infinite detail amid masses of lengthy laws.

In contrast to all this Christ stands among men and declares, "I am truth." In him there was not a particle of hypocrisy. He had no false front, no duplicity, no double talk. It was this characteristic of utter truthfulness which so enraged the hypocritical Pharisees and ecclesiastical intelligentsia of his day.

As a matter of fact it is his utter honesty, his absolute veracity, which all through history has alienated dishonest and insincere people. The double-dealers and cunning contrivers have

31

always tried to belittle, deny, and even destroy the truth expressed in the character of Christ. They have done this simply because he made them so uncomfortable. Little wonder they crucified Jesus; no less wonder he is still scorned.

But for the man or woman who wants security, who seeks serenity, who is searching for someone to really trust, he still stands waiting quietly. He is no different now than he was when he tramped over the bare, brown, sun-baked hills of Palestine. Whenever a soul, soured and scarred by betrayed trust in other people, turns to him, it finds truth and integrity and utter honesty.

We see this drama depicted over and over in the day-to-day incidents of his life. Men and women whose lives were nightmares of agony, whose hearts had been broken by betrayed love, whose tensions and anxieties were destroying their most cherished relationships, came to Christ and found fresh hope and new life. What is more, they found rest for the simple reason they had found someone on whom they could rely.

We can well understand what an amazing experience it must have been for ordinary human beings to meet the Christ, who was totally truthful and absolutely honest. It was akin to stumbling on an oasis with clear bubbling springs of truth amid the dreadful desolation of a vast desert of dishonesty.

Is it any wonder that poor prostitutes, crude fishermen, ordinary children, and cunning tax collectors were captivated by Christ and came to consider him their closest friend? But beyond all this, they learned to love him dearly.

What happened then still happens today. When any person is prepared to come to Christ in open, honest humility, without pretense or sham, he at once finds a friend. There is an immediate response from our own inner spirit to the Spirit of truth apparent in the person of Jesus Christ. There is an attraction which is generated through our finding someone worthy of our utmost confidence and trust. There is nothing in life so calculated to relieve tension and strain as knowing there is a friend available to whom we can turn in every situation.

Best of all are the quiet assurance and very comforting knowledge that Christ never does betray the confidence we put in him. He never does let us down. He never does doublecross us. He never plays us false.

Next to the truthfulness and utter integrity of Christ, perhaps his most important characteristic is his strength. This may seem a strange thing to say, for far too often he has been depicted as rather a frail figure. Well-intentioned but grossly misleading descriptions of him such as "gentle Jesus, meek and mild" have done God an enormous disservice.

Not for a moment do I deny that Christ was one of the world's truly great gentlemen. Nor do I wish to detract in any way from his amazing humility and utter graciousness. But he was no milquetoast. Nor was he a shaky-kneed weakling. Nor did he ever cringe or cower in the presence of terrible pressures put upon him. Rather he stands as a great mountain of divine manhood completely overshadowing and overtowering both his contemporaries and all subsequent geniuses.

Actually one of the terrible injustices the Christian church has done to Christ's character is its attempt to confine him to a merely human concept. Too often he is portrayed as a pathetic babe in arms, an emaciated, white-faced, feeble man, a broken corpse on Calvary's cross, or even worse, a plastercast character with a halo around his head.

Many of these impressions of the person of Christ have come down to us through the centuries. They have been conveyed to us in unrealistic art, rather insipid writings, distorted pageantry, and the peculiar patterns of human thought whereby we attempt to reduce the Lord of the Universe to the level of our own frail flesh.

33

It is highly important, therefore, for us to take another look at Jesus Christ in the context of his own behavior among us. There is little value in merely stating that being God, he is all-powerful, all-wise, and so on. Before we can believe this we must see for ourselves he could really live life in the rough-and-tumble world of men and be in complete control of every situation he encountered.

After all we must remind ourselves that he said not only, "I am the truth," but also, "I am the way, and the truth, and the life." In other words, he was demonstrating how to live life in a way which embodied enormous dignity, strength, and quiet assurance.

Those of us who think hard and deeply about the difficulties of society have long since realized that one of its major problems is the basic insecurity of people. As time goes on, men and women seem less and less able to cope with the complexities of their own society. There is an uneasy feeling that things are out of control and one can do very little about it. No one seems to have the answers, and if a solution is found for one problem, a dozen new ones spring up in its place.

Against such a bizarre and bewildering background it comes as a tremendous tonic and inspiration for us to discover someone who has the answers. It is an enormous uplift to find in Christ a character of such unusual strength that he is able to cope readily with every exigency of life. What is even more remarkable, we find here a person whose character is of such force and dynamic power that he not only copes with but actually controls and directs all events.

Always, always, we must think of Christ and see him as the "one in control," the "one in charge," the "one in command." He was not a victim of circumstances. He was not a pawn on the chessboard of life, pushed about and manipulated at will.

From his boyhood to his ascension we stand in awe at the strong, quiet, superior way in which Christ moved through life. In the temple at the age of twelve he was already able to hold the attention of much older men steeped in the Scriptures of his people. In the carpenter's shop he was the craftsman with skill enough to earn an adequate livelihood for his widowed mother and younger siblings. In fact by the time he was thirty he must have set aside sufficient savings to provide for his family's welfare while he went away on his public ministry.

We see him, strong in body, toughened by toil, browned by the sun, starting off towards the Jordan to be publicly baptized by John the Baptist. At once he is recognized by that great mystic as a man apart, one whose shoe latchets the Baptist is unworthy to unfasten. Here is a giant among his contemporaries, and John makes no bones about it.

Instinctively, rugged young men are attracted to Jesus Christ. The majority of his followers are in their late teens or early twenties. They are attracted by the strength, the courage, the purpose of this person. He epitomizes their highest aspirations. Willingly they turn away from their assorted trades to tramp the endless sun-scorched miles with him.

For nearly three years the hearty band will share their meals and beds beneath open skies. It takes stamina and vigor and vitality to live like this, where each soon discovers all the strengths and weaknesses of his fellows. Here there can be no sham, no false front, no coverup. And Christ lived this way, calling his companions "friends," despite all the times they disappointed him.

We see Christ alone in the desert, dealing with the devil. We see him handle that crafty character with such consummate skill and strength that the "old snake" is soon on the run.

We see him in the storms that blow up with such frequency on the Lake of Galilee. He but speaks a word and the winds die, the waves subside. Here is one totally in control of even the basic physical elements, just as he is utterly in control of spiritual powers.

This Christ could turn water to wine, just as he could turn sinning men and women into saints. He could take a boy's small buns and bless them to feed thousands of famished people. In the same way he could take a handful of spiritual food and break it down to simple truth able to satisfy a thousand hungry hearts.

It takes strength of spirit, toughness of mind, and immense moral insight to achieve these results. It doesn't just happen. It happens only when the basic ingredients for achieving miracles are held in the control of one with unusual capacities. And never has a character of comparable stature stepped upon the world scene. Like all great geniuses, he achieved what he did without fanfare or show.

We find him confronted with disease, death, and even decay of human flesh. None of these deter him. He does not try to avoid them or evade the demands they put upon him. Instead he deals with them deftly and convincingly. The blind see; the deaf hear; the dumb speak; the lepers are cured; the lame walk; the dead are raised; the forces of decomposition are reversed.

This was not mass hypnotism. It was not black magic. It was not witchcraft or mind over matter. It was the strength of one in harmony with his Father, simply demonstrating his enormous power on behalf of others.

We see Jesus Christ approaching Calvary. We see him deliberately choose to die, the just one in place of the guilty ones. We see him not as a martyr but a a quiet monarch deciding his own end. Despite the trumped-up charges, despite the kangaroo court, despite the scheming and knavery of his accusers, we see this strong one emerge from the ordeal unscathed and unsullied. Always he is in charge of events.

Even on the cross, amid appalling agony, he is able to grant pardon to his accusers and look with love upon his mother, commending her to another's care. It takes a giant of a character to so conduct oneself, and Christ was just that.

At last we see him triumph over death. We see him shatter the shackles of the grave. We see him ascend to be seated in honor and splendor and might at his Father's right hand. None other ever deserved such exaltation. None other has ever demonstrated such fortitude and strength of character to attain it.

So I say that it is no small thing to have our confidence in Christ, the living Lord. To know that we have someone of this caliber to whom we may entrust ourselves in every situation is to have found one of the great secrets to serene living.

Here is one always in control. Here is one able to meet any exigency in life. Here is one with the answers to every dilemma.

What a friend to find! What a companion in whom we may put our confidence. What a one to take control of our affairs and our lives—if we will let him.

This leads us to consider the next amazing aspect of Christ's character—namely, his approachability. Notwithstanding his utter truthfulness and his magnificent strength, there is something immensely warm and endearing about Christ. He is not a far-off God ensconced somewhere in the distant skies. Nor is he a dusty, ancient historical character obscured in the haze of antiquity. Nor is he a stern, august adjudicator standing afar in dour judgment. Nor is he merely a mysterious mystic.

He is Jesus, the Christ, with the common touch for common men. He is the suffering Savior who was a man of sorrows and acquainted with grief—our sort of grief. He did not come to condemn the world but to redeem it; He did not come to judge us but to lift us up. His main mission was to bind up the brokenhearted, to set free captives, to comfort all that mourn, to give beauty in place of ashes and the oil of joy and garment of praise in place of heavy spirits.

Is it any marvel men and women come to him? Is it any wonder that people learn to love him so dearly?

4

The Love of God

I n one way it would have been better to entitle this chapter "The God of Love." I say this because in contemplating the character of God, as seen in Christ, we are immediately impressed by his unparalleled love.

If by chance anyone thinks of God apart from and outside of the context of love, then it is fairly safe to say he really does not know him. For, of all God's attributes, none is so apparent as his love. It completely overshadows all of the integrity, strength, humility, and approachability discussed in the previous chapter. Basically it was the love in Christ's life which drew men and women to him. It was his completely open selflessness which made such an enormous impact on the people of his time.

Before we can understand this we must grasp the true significance of God's love. We must understand and appreciate what sort of love it is. We cannot equate it with the types of so-called love which are commonly referred to in our human language, especially in the English idiom.

Throughout the Scriptures reference is made to three kinds of love. The first I shall mention is that of a purely physical nature. It is the mutual response between male and female. It is what the modern world and modern men and women think of immediately when the word *love* is mentioned. Unfortunately it has been reduced to little more than mere sex. Yet in Scripture it is still a sublime relationship between two people, each of whom has committed himself completely to the other. It is part of God's profound planning for parenthood, and in its proper setting provides human beings with an enormous sense of security and serenity within the sanctuary of a home.

The second sort of love dealt with in Scripture is commonly referred to as filial love. It is the deep devotion and affection which can grow between brothers and sisters, parents and children, mutual friends, members of the same community, or even men and women caught up in a common cause; for example, in battle, servicemen will actually lay down their lives for their comrades, or men engaged in research or exploration or adventure will readily risk themselves for the welfare of their companions.

This love is lodged in the realm of our minds and emotions. It is born through close and continuous contact of men and women in any given situation. It may commence with the most casual acquaintance, grow into mutual respect or admiration, and finally flower in the full-blown reality of an abiding and enduring affection.

The third kind of love spoken of in Scripture is the love of God. It is love in its deepest and most profound spiritual sense. This is a sort of love which few people know much about. It is a love totally transcending the other two.

This love is, for want of a better definition, absolute self-less-ness. It is the spirit of always putting others' interests ahead of one's own. It is the inner attitude of laying oneself out at any cost for others, even one's enemies. Actually it implies giving up one's own rights and prerogatives in order to be completely available to others. In short, it is death to self.

It is precisely at this point where we find that this love is essential to a life free from tension and anxiety. I say this simply because anyone who experiences it in a personal contact with Christ is suddenly set free from the anxieties attached to ordinary human love at its lower levels.

In the very nature of things we soon discover in life that in order to be loved either in a physical or filial dimension we must show ourselves lovable. Somehow we have to demonstrate to others that we are worth loving. We have to prove that we are worthy of their love. And, sad to say, in most cases, the moment we fail to do this we discover that we are being cut off. The very fact that we may fail to live up to the expectations of others may induce them to lose interest in us; their confidence is shaken; they may feel a bit betrayed and so their love to us dries up.

This explains why families break up. It explains why husbands and wives separate. It explains why brothers and sisters or parents and children may become deeply alienated and antagonistic. It explains why the best of friends may become the worst of enemies. It explains why in society as a whole there is the endless fret over offending others. It explains why so many people live under constant tension trying to hold their homes together. It explains the feverish fear of losing friends and making enemies.

Now, amazing as it may sound, and incredible as it may seem, there is none of this in the love of God. The simple truth is that his love for me does not in any way depend on my worthiness of it. In other words, I do not have to merit his love. I do not, so to speak, have to earn his love.

Scripture repeats this theme again and again. For example, in that most poignant of all the stories told by Jesus, the account of the prodigal son, we see clearly portrayed for us what the love of God is like. In fact Christ used this parable to convey concisely what is meant by God's love.

Here was a young man who deliberately chose to squander his father's hard-won earnings. He was a strong-willed, selfish young upstart who set out to live it up, no matter what the consequences. Not only did he heap shame upon himself but he also dragged his father's reputation into disgrace. More than that he knowingly grieved the dear old man and broke his heart with anxiety.

In the normal course of events, especially in the Middle East, such a son would have been long since disowned. He would have been disinherited. He would have been banished forever from the home.

But in one of the most poignant word pictures ever painted, Christ shows the father's reaction when his prodigal son turns toward home. He runs to him. He embraces him. He kisses him. He brushes aside his protestations of unworthiness. He puts a new, clean cloak around him, fresh shoes on his feet, a ring on his finger. The feast is prepared. This is the love of God.

No doubt the dear old man had died a thousand deaths after his son's departure. Without question he had been humiliated into the dust by the damaging reports that came back to him of his son's conduct. Certainly his hair must have turned gray and his eyes red with weeping as he wondered what would become of his son.

Yet his attitude of devotion, affection, and utter selflessness never altered. It mattered not what happened to himself as long as his son could be restored and redeemed and remade. His care and concern for this one's welfare never abated.

This is the love of God.

This is utter selflessness.

This is total self-sacrifice.

Little marvel, then, that men and women who have encountered this sort of love are set free from fear. For the first time in life they have found a love so great, so magnanimous, so generous it does not depend on their behavior or their worthiness. Rather, it is expressed simply because it is in fact a very part of God himself. It is his own inherent character. For as John the beloved apostle wrote so emphatically, *"God is love."*

The truly thrilling and wonderful release that attends an encounter with Christ is something which has to be experienced before it can be fully appreciated. For the first time one is set free from the fear and worry of not being worthy, of not being lovable, of not deserving such love. Instead there comes the calm, quiet delight of knowing I am loved simply because Christ loves me, God loves me!

Trying to put this on paper in mere human language is an almost impossible endeavor. I am here dealing with a subject of such enormous spiritual significance that it will scarcely submit to such simple treatment as I have given it. Still the fact remains that for those few who have found the love of God, life is never quite the same again.

Once this love has swept into their spirits it replaces the old stagnant hates, fears, worries, prejudices, and fret with its own pure stream. Attitudes alter. We begin to see others in a new light and in a new way. Our entire outlook on others changes. We find the statement made by Paul in 2 Timothy 1:7 to be an absolute reality, "For God hath not given us a spirit of fear; but of power, and of love, and of a sound [disciplined] mind."

Or to put it as John does, "We love him, because he first loved us" (1 John 4:19). And to our own astonishment we find that our love both to God himself and to others is intensified. Perhaps previously we may not have so much as given God more than a casual passing thought. Suddenly, now, Christ becomes to us the dearest friend. We actually take delight in living to please him. His incredible love extended to us in spite of our unworthiness elicits an enthusiastic and spontaneous response from us so now we do endeavor deliberately to live worthy of such a one.

Likewise in our relationship with others. No longer do we stand in judgment of their every action and attitude. Instead, broken and humbled by the love of God given to us, we turn to our fellow human beings and extend the same compassion to them.

The whole question of forgiveness follows the same lines. It has amazed me to discover how many people live under tension because of unforgiven issues in their lives. Either they themselves feel unforgiven or they hold grudges and grievances against others, refusing to grant forgiveness for some wrong or injury they may have suffered. How often we hear the bitter remark, "I will never forgive them for it," or, "I will never forgive myself for behaving in the way I did."

Now it is quite impossible for anyone to have such an attitude and experience serenity. A lack of forgiveness generates tensions and anxieties at the very deepest levels of human experience. Nothing can be more insidious than the inner turmoil of an unforgiving or unforgiven spirit.

We humans are past masters at the art of self-deception. All too often we simply assume rather naively that time will take care of such tensions. We try to shrug them off. We attempt to dismiss them from our lives or bury them in forgetfulness. But unfortunately if we can't forgive, we can't forget. So the old animosity or alienation rankles deep within our spirits like a worm boring through a beautiful fruit. Unless, ultimately, the matter is resolved, the entire life can be blighted.

In our relationship to God most of us stagger along through life with the same sort of apprehensions. We are quite sure our conduct does not meet with his approval. We sense a certain degree of guilt because of our misdeeds. In our better moments we wish we could do better. But on the whole we really wonder if we can be forgiven our faults and failings.

All of this is very disconcerting. Certainly it cannot contribute to a quiet and contented spirit. But at the same time few people know how their dilemma can be resolved.

I recall vividly an experience of this kind with a dear lady who suffered from Parkinson's disease. She had regularly attended church. But it was quite obvious that just going to services and listening to sermons had not solved the inner tensions which tormented her. Most of her difficulties revolved around the question of forgiveness.

One morning, sitting quietly beside me on the sofa in her living room, she began to unburden herself to me. "Do you really think, Mr. Keller," she said, looking deep into my eyes, "that God can really forgive me for all my past?" She was not an emotional woman. Her eyes were hard and piercing and very searching as she asked the stabbing question.

Instead of answering her from my own background I asked her to turn to the story of the prodigal boy. Together we read through Luke 15:11–20. When we read that the lad's father saw him coming, had compassion, and ran to embrace him, I turned and said, "You see, the father never stopped loving him. He *was* forgiven before he ever got back!" There was a pause between us of several moments' silence.

She turned to me and said softly, "You mean God, my Father, has already forgiven me?"

"Yes," I replied gently, "You are forgiven! All you have to do is accept the forgiveness."

She suddenly snatched up a box of Kleenex and the tissues tumbled out one after another as she tried to stanch the stream of tears that flooded from her eyes.

"Don't feel bad, Mr. Keller!" she exclaimed. "They are tears of pure joy—pure joy. I have been forgiven. I *am* forgiven!"

Such is the liberation of a spirit set free from the tormenting tensions of guilt, self-accusation, and feeling unforgiven. And may I add, only the man or woman who knows such release is in turn able to extend complete and wholehearted forgiveness to fellow human beings.

On the surface this may all seem quite simple. And in a sense it is. God, in Christ, has been good enough to make our contacts and relationship with him simple and uncomplicated, so much so that even a small child or the most untutored savage can come. Still this does not detract from the drastic and deeply profound measures taken by God himself, in love, to make this possible.

I say this lest the reader assume that God is so soft and sentimental that he merely overlooks our faults and more or less winks at our misconduct.

Just the opposite is so. Being who he is, not only loving and merciful and forgiving, but also strong, honest, just, and utterly righteous, he cannot tolerate our misdeeds. Most of us in our more somber moments will admit to ourselves, if not to others, that we are not deserving of his love. We know instinctively that we ought to suffer the penalty for our own perverseness. We sense a real wretchedness in the presence of Christ's own impeccable character. Yet wonder of wonders, he does not demand or insist on retribution for our misconduct. *Why?*

Because he himself bore the penalty for our faults and failures and unforgiving spirits at Calvary. It was he who suffered in my stead. This is essentially the significance of the cross.

It is surprising how many people miss this point completely. Somehow they seem to insist all through life on trying to atone for their own misbehavior. Such an attitude keeps them under constant stress. They are always afraid that they might not be able to quite make it to heaven. They are anxious and worried lest their bad behavior outweigh their charitable deeds. So they stagger through life carrying a depressing load of anxiety. These strains and stresses are not figments of their imagination; they are very real tensions which can work havoc with both their mental and physical well-being.

But, on the other hand, when we come to Christ, or, if you wish, come home to our heavenly Father in simplicity, these tensions are immediately tamed. First we suddenly see that we are in fact loved by God our Father despite our misdeeds. Then we discover that we are forgiven despite all the damage we have done, and finally it dawns upon us that he is the one who has borne the cost of our misconduct at his own expense on Calvary.

Really all that is required is for me to accept these facts. The moment I do, a tremendous sense of emancipation sweeps through my spirit. I am set free! All the old gnawing guilt, anxieties, and tensions are gone. And at last it is possible to relax and feel at home with God, for in fact that is exactly what has happened. I have come home to my heavenly Father.

Once this happens to us, and we know the intoxicating delight of having been set free, suddenly our attitude to others alters. It is quite impossible for anyone who has sensed his own forgiveness by God to go out and harbor grudges against another person. This is perhaps a shocking statement to make. It needs to be made with emphasis. For the degree to which I sense and appreciate God's forgiveness to me in very large measure determines how willing I am to forgive others. By the same measurement, the depth to which I feel and perceive the love of God my Father for me decides exactly how much compassion and concern I can bear towards others.

There is no substitute for love and forgiveness and compassionate human understanding to ease friction and reduce the strains and stresses which arise between human beings. And when I pause to reflect that God, who knows the worst about me, is still willing to love, forgive, and cherish me, then there is a strong stimulus for me to extend the same treatment to others.

As I grow to be an older man and look back down the long trail of my life, perhaps the most poignant thought which comes to me again and again is the unrelenting love of God to me and his unlimited forgiveness despite all my failures. Nothing so warms my heart toward him. Nothing so stimulates my spirit with hope and zest. And may I add, nothing else so induces me to extend a measure of compassion, love, and forgiveness to my fellows on the tough trail of life. It helps ease the strain on all of us.

I wish to point out and emphasize that this magnanimous attitude towards others represents no special merit, no particular good on my part. It does not even have its origin with me. Rather it is the result of the inflow of God's Spirit and life into my life. It is the passing on to others of the love, compassion, forgiveness, and sympathetic understanding extended to me by God.

This in itself produces both in me and in others a relaxed sense of goodwill. It banishes the old behavior patterns of bitterness, hate, and tension that torment us. Added to all this is a lighthearted freedom from the old nagging fears that taunt those who have never felt forgiven or are unable to forgive. Life becomes a cheerful adventure instead of a drab ordeal because one can be utterly open, honest, and fully available to others.

After all, this is precisely what God himself has done for us in Christ at Calvary and what Christ now continues to do as the living, exalted Lord. He is always laying himself out for us. He is always making himself available to us by his own gracious Spirit. He is ever coming to us in heartwarming affection. He is ever reassuring us of his love, his concern, his forgiveness, his interest in our welfare.

All of this is part and parcel of the love of God. Such love is so utterly foreign to so many that they can scarcely believe it to be true. This is complete selflessness and self-sacrifice in contradistinction to our usual human selfishness. Wherever it touches our lives and enters our hearts, it begins its own wondrous work of transformation.

5

Belonging to God's Family

rom our earliest years all of us instinctively crave to belong to a group. We yearn to be a part of a social community. Because of our very makeup, most of us are most comfortable, most at ease, most relaxed in the company of others who accept us as one of their own.

We find, for example, that tiny tots become very uneasy and tense the moment they are cut off from the comfort and companionship of Mother and Dad. Every growing child finds a certain degree of confidence and assurance by belonging to a family. And, if by some upheaval the family is fractured and divided, its members undergo enormous stresses and strains.

It is common knowledge that young people who are exposed to the anxieties inherent in broken homes become very insecure. Somehow they seem to fear that even worse tragedies can overtake them at any time. They become suspicious of others and tend to build high walls of self-defense around themselves to protect their lives from further suffering.

Any person who at any time has been rejected by a group to which he belonged carries a certain stigma of failure and frustration. He may make repeated attempts to prove himself in order to become accepted again. It is surprising the lengths to which some will go in order to become identified with a group. This explains much teenage behavior. And if teens don't make it into the group and are spurned, we find them retreating still deeper within their own walled fortress.

These patterns of behavior persist all through life. The upshot is that many people are under tremendous tension simply because they do not feel they have succeeded in "belonging." In a strange way thousands of otherwise normal people feel that they are really not wanted. They may have a few casual friends or acquaintances, but still they are haunted with the painful, persistent pangs of loneliness.

The number of people who live with this sort of distress grows steadily in society. It is actually a most disquieting experience to discover firsthand just how many human beings there are who actually feel unloved, unwanted, and uncared for. They are very much alone. Life is a trial. More than that, it is a dreadful bore.

There are a number of reasons why this spirit of heaviness is spreading all through Western society. The breakup of homes alienates and divides hundreds of thousands of people. Men, women, and children feel deserted, abandoned, rejected, and unwanted. The increase in urban living has brought millions into metropolitan areas where on the surface one would imagine they could never get lonely. But a great city can be the most lonely and forbidding spot on earth. There may be hundreds of human beings around you, not one of whom cares a whit what happens to you. Coupled with city life is the modern mania to be on the move. People drift hither and yon without putting down roots. They don't belong anywhere. There is the eternal difficulty of trying to make new friends and to find someone who shows an interest in you. Finally there is old age, which medical service tends to prolong.

Often the twilight years are the most tormenting simply because one's friends and family die and depart; the younger generation is frequently so preoccupied with its own affairs that younger people find little time for the aged. More than this, old age is often beset with all sorts of stress and anxiety as one's powers and ability to cope with changing events are less effective.

So the questions have to be asked, and asked in a frank, forthright manner, "Is there an antidote for this tension of loneliness? Is there some spiritual stimulant to counteract the spirit of heaviness apparent in so many lives?"

Happily I can say yes. And I can say so with great emphasis.

It will have become apparent to the reader by this time that if one has a direct and personal encounter with God by his Spirit, some basic changes will be bound to take place in life. Of these perhaps the most beautiful, and certainly the most winsome, is the growing awareness that I am part of a new community. There steals over my spirit the assurance that I have been accepted. I sense in a strangely moving way that somehow now I do belong.

Actually what has happened is that God is no longer a distant, abstract concept on the far horizon of my life. Instead he has come close in the comforting and wonderfully reassuring role of my Father.

For my part, I am no longer just a nonentity of no consequence amid the mass of humanity. Suddenly I have become a child of God, an individual in whom my heavenly Father is personally interested. Not only is he interested in me as his child, but also he is deeply concerned about every detail of my life. This means that I am now free to turn to him about any matter that might arise, knowing that I shall get a sympathetic hearing.

Such a relationship immediately sets me free from tensions which could torment me. First of all, it is wonderful to belong to him and know I am wanted. Secondly, it is thrilling to sense that someone is sufficiently interested in my affairs to give me sympathetic attention.

In addition to this I find in Christ, God's other Son, not only a Savior, but also a friend and brother. He himself used these terms, so I make no apologies for doing the same. He invites me to share with him all the events of my life.

It is this ready acceptability that makes our relationship so real and meaningful. It requires no special ritual, no ornate sanctuary, no ecclesiastical hierarchy or priesthood for me to present him with my petitions. I simply come on the spur of the moment and tell him all about my affairs. He enjoys knowing about my good times just as much as he wants to sympathize with my difficulties. And we do him a distinct disservice if we dump only our troubles in his lap. After all, he wants to rejoice with me just as much as he is willing to weep with me.

I have purposely avoided using the word *prayer* up to this point in the book simply because for so many it smacks of musty churches, mournful music, and boring rituals. But basically, true prayer is simply a quiet, sincere, genuine conversation with God. It is a two-way dialogue between friends.

Of course the moment I mention prayer a good many people may feel a bit put off. After all, they assume, this is some sort of pious exercise performed almost as a painful penance by priests, preachers, and other plaster-cast recluses.

Genuine prayer is nothing of the sort. It is the heartfelt impression of my spirit finding expression in such a way that it elicits a response from the Spirit of God. For both my heavenly

Father and Christ my Savior do speak to me by the Spirit. He is the one who conveys to me in a still, small, inner voice the thoughts, impulses, and intentions of God. He does this both directly with distinct impressions upon my spirit and indirectly through outer influences such as the advice of godly friends, the trend of current circumstances, the reading of Scripture, or even the natural phenomena of the world around me.

No matter how or when a conversation is carried on within the family of God, it continually convinces and reassures me of the presence and approachability of my heavenly Father. Few relationships in life can be as heartening and inspiring as this. It is the great elixir of life. No longer do I live on the common level. I sense that I have been lifted up into a new dimension of living in which I actually walk and talk with God my Father and his Son my Brother. My earthly sojourn is not just a barren, boring existence dragged on from day to day of unbearable loneliness and pointlessness. Now it becomes a bright adventure with each new day charged with eager anticipation.

It needs to be made clear that this sort of close and intimate relationship with God does not just happen in a moment, so to speak. Just as with a human relationship, it requires time and care to cultivate this cherished family life. Too many of us turn to God only in times of trouble or grief. This is a selfish way to treat him. If we want to be generous and give him some joy, then surely we can be big enough to share our sanguine, happy moments with him as well.

A fact few people realize is that it is possible to give God great joy. It is one of the ways we can demonstrate to him that we do truly appreciate all that he does for us. It proves beyond doubt that we don't take him for granted. Throughout Scripture, this is referred to as "praising him." But the word *praise* is gradually changing in meaning. Nowadays when we speak of praising a person the idea that springs to mind is one of flattery or commendation. But God our Father does not want either our flattery or a pat on the back. What he really wants and deeply appreciates is our genuine gratitude.

Because of this I do not hesitate to say that the person who has learned to live in an "attitude of gratitude" for all God's benefits has found one of the great secrets to successful spiritual living. Nothing pleases God more than our deep appreciation for all that he has done and all that he is. We soon discover that just as there is great tranquility in a human family where appreciation is frequently expressed, so the same is true in the family of God. Try it and you will find your days are full of delight rather than drabness.

It is my personal conviction that faith and gratitude go hand in hand. If anything, one could say that gratitude grows out of faith. It is the expression of appreciation for confidence vindicated.

In our relationships both with God and others it is beautiful to see how gratitude generates confidence and confidence honored, in turn, produces gratitude. And when these both function harmoniously in our everyday experiences we find ourselves set free from much of the frustration and fretting that make up the fever of living.

It is a tremendous tonic for a mere mortal to know that he is in personal contact with the immortal. And when such a contact is continuous it gradually dawns upon him that he, too, is partaking of this same immortality. Put in another way, once I find myself a member of God's family, I realize that a very real rebirth has occurred. I have been remade. My attitudes alter, my outlook on life is redirected, and my entire conduct takes on a new tenor.

Probably the most significant aspect of this new relationship is an overwhelming sense of genuine gratitude to God for what has happened. Coupled with this is a keen awareness of having been set free from the old fears and anxieties. It is possible now to relax and enjoy the benefits bestowed on me without worrying about trying to earn them or merit some special favor through adhering to rigid rules.

The Scriptures, of course, state that this should be so. But few people seem to express proper gratitude. Yet when I truly realize what privileges have been bestowed on me in becoming God's child, there is bound to be enormous gratitude.

This gratitude finds expression in many ways. It is a continuous appreciation for all that Christ has achieved for me by his life, death, resurrection, and teaching. It is a genuine thankfulness for the presence and guidance of God's Spirit. It is a never-failing delight over knowing God as my Father and his knowing me as his child.

All of this gives enormous impetus to the human spirit. But it also goes far beyond just the spiritual realm. We become keenly aware that every good thing which we enjoy has had its origin with God. All the events of life take on special significance because we are aware that they are part of our Father's plan and purpose for us, his blueprint for us.

As I live in this "attitude of gratitude," even the most ordinary things become sublime. The common world around me becomes diffused with the divine. The sunrise I watched break in crimson splendor above the purple sea this morning speaks to me of his beauty and majesty. The call of the cuckoo from a nearby tree and the flight of a tiny wren remind me of his care even for birds. The steady fall of raindrops on the window and fragrance of fresh earth tell of his faithfulness in supplying sufficient moisture for all the vegetation of grass, trees, shrubs, and flowers. The smile playing upon the contented face of my wife and the shining sparkle in her warm brown eyes are a reminder of the great joys given again and again to his children.

In all of this there comes refreshment of spirit. It is like a clear, pure stream of godly gratitude that flushes away fear and foreboding, tension and strain. And life becomes beautiful when I belong to God's family.

This does not imply that there will be no troubles in life. It does not mean that there will be no gray days, no suffering, no sorrow, no tough times. But what it does mean is that no matter what comes I am better able to cope because I am in good company and I know there is someone close at hand who is deeply concerned and cares how I am getting along. This is the precious part about belonging to God's family.

Then, too, we discover that other ordinary human beings just like ourselves have become members of this same family. We sense a common bond that binds us all together. In this fraternity there are also new strength and friendship which are refreshing to our spirits. This bond unites men and women from diverse backgrounds, races, and strata of society as no other fellowship upon earth can do.

I recall clearly one day when I was somewhat lonely on a rather remote island in the mid-Pacific. For a number of reasons a mood of melancholy had settled over my spirit so that even the loveliness of the sea and the brilliance of the sunshine could not seem to rouse me. As I strolled alone along the shore, I was approached by an elderly Japanese gentleman. He smiled politely, bowed, and engaged me in casual conversation.

After a few minutes our discussion turned to deeper subjects. Soon I found he was a gracious man with a great confidence in Christ. As brothers we shared our common love for God and his for us. In a matter of an hour my spirit was singing and soaring in gratitude for this one who had crossed my path. Such are the benefits of belonging to God's family.

6

Contented Living

ne of the earmarks of any person who has come into a viable and meaningful relationship with God as his heavenly Father is an attitude of quiet contentment with life. Gone are the emptiness and frustration of a pointless existence. In its place there are purpose and meaning and direction in all one does.

The above is a fairly easy statement to make on paper. The reader may pass over it almost unnoticed. But to encounter it in actual life and to find people of whom it is true is another thing. There are, in fact, very few such fortunate people. I say this simply because of the general discontent of our age.

Despite our ever-increasing affluence, despite our shorter workweeks, despite our greater leisure, despite our increased longevity, despite our more advanced technology, despite our improved social benefits, men and women are today probably more restless, more uneasy, and more discontented than ever before. Life for most seems to be a strained state of apprehension and tension. They seem to be caught up in an ever-accelerating stream of events over which they have little or no control. They are swept along on the swirling current of circumstances which leaves them dazed and bewildered.

Repeatedly we hear such remarks as, "Well, I certainly don't know where we are headed," or, "There just seems to be nothing one can do to change events," or, "We seem to have lost control of our own affairs and are just drifting toward disaster," or even more emphatically, "I'd hate to be around twenty years from now!"

All of this gives expression to the deep inner dissatisfaction with life. It betrays the anxiety and gnawing worries which plague so many people. It demonstrates the dilemma and dismay of those who really wonder what life is all about. Above all it gives emphasis to the general fever of human discontent and weariness with the world.

This is a most wearing way to live. It erodes away the zest for living. It robs men and women of quiet serenity. It denies them the great calm assurance of knowing where they are going.

But once we have come into contact with Christ and recognize the great honors and privileges bestowed on us in being God's children this all changes. Probably the most astonishing alteration that takes place in our outlook is our overall attitude towards life itself and the world in general. Instead of these few years of our sojourn upon the planet earth being the great end in itself, we see it as the means to an even greater end. We discover that life is for learning, learning how better to love God and love our fellow men and love all that is worthwhile in the world.

Actually this learning to love is just another way of saying we are here to learn how to really live as our Father wishes us to live—not for self and selfish reasons, but for others, for God, and for causes much greater than ourselves. Only the person who gives his life to something or someone much greater than his own small self can ever sense the surge of God's Spirit sweeping into his spirit, catching him up in the great, eternal, ongoing purposes of God himself.

We simply have to remember that though men and nations may be bewildered, bored, and weary with world events, God our Father is not. Despite all the circumstances which may appear contrary to his ideals, he is still very much in control of human history. He knows precisely what he is doing with his planet and the people on it. His purposes are being fulfilled and realized down to the most minute detail.

In view of this it is downright exciting for his dear children to have a part in seeing all his program accomplished. We become actively engaged in his activities. We see ourselves playing a part that is both helpful and constructive amid a society which is otherwise chaotic and destructive. Instead of standing on the sidelines we sense that we are very much in the stream of events, so to speak. We see ourselves making a worthwhile contribution of enduring consequence in God's overall strategy.

This immediately gives positive direction to our living. It lends special significance to what we do, no matter how trivial our little common round may be. Because we are tied into and linked up with the mighty purposes of God, even our most mundane affairs take on rich meaning. All of this contributes great contentment to our individual days. Life is not just a waste of time now but a use of time for a great cause.

This is why the beloved Brother Lawrence could write in his memoirs that it was possible for him to even pick up a straw from the ground or do dishes in the drab kitchen and do it for God his father. The most trivial task can thus take on a touch of eternal worth.

Learning to live this way and to love this way is really a matter of maturing and growing up in God's family. Gradually as we go on there steal over us subtle but splendid changes in character. We may not be aware of these alterations ourselves, but others around us are.

What is actually happening to us is that we are gradually being conformed to the character and likeness of Christ. As we invite his Spirit to come into our careers and into our lives we find that he there tends to produce his own characteristics in us. Instead of being tense and anxious and nervous we become more clam, confident, and relaxed. This is because we become increasingly aware that just as God our Father is very much in control of outer events in the world around us, he can likewise be in calm control of the inner turmoil of the world within us.

Essentially this is what we mean by allowing ourselves to be led or guided by God. It is what we refer to as being under Christ's control. It is the thought of my spirit's being so in harmony with God's Spirit that there is a desire and willingness to do God's will.

This really is not half as mysterious or mystical as it may sound. Knowing and doing the will of God baffle a lot of well-intentioned people. They are very happy to become God's children. They are delighted to find their misconduct forgiven. They are often very happy to sense the joy of God's companionship and are more than ready to help his cause along, but, and it is a big "but," doing his will, that's different.

I feel it is very significant that the degree of contentment apparent in most lives is directly proportional to the degree in which they are doing God's will. It is akin to the old saying that "our own happiness is exactly proportional to our helpfulness."

The person who senses deep down inside that he is living and moving and acting in accord with the wishes of his heavenly Father has found the secret to sublime and serene life. He has stepped out of the swamp and quagmire of confused experiences onto the high road of solid and straightforward walking with God.

Now life is no longer an enigma. It is the way home. This world is not the last word. It is but a part of the path that prepares me for a much wider realm of life to come. Even death is not to be dreaded. It is but the doorway through which I step into a new dimension of living.

If we pause briefly to examine Christ's life on earth, we will readily see all of these attitudes in his outlook. From the beginning to the end Jesus continually emphasized and reemphasized that he was here doing his Father's will, saying what he would say, working in the way he would work. Always he reiterated and held before himself the great joy and anticipation of going home. It is moving to study Christ's life and note how often he spoke of going to his Father. With all this in view, it is little wonder he could face Calvary and death with fortitude. Beyond the grave he knew there lay the incredible and wonderful realm of a still wider life. So, though his outer circumstances may have been tempestuous, his inner life was supremely content.

Because Jesus Christ lived and moved always in accord with the will of his Father, we see him striding across the pages of history with a strength and dignity and purpose unmatched by any other character. Because his spirit was in harmony with the Spirit of God, we see him achieving every aim and accomplishing every purpose for which he came to earth. In spite of what seemed utter disaster and defeat to his contemporaries, he emerges ultimately as the greatest victor over evil for all time. Notwithstanding circumstances and surroundings which would have broken and shattered anyone else, he stands strong and supreme, a character of enormous vitality and quiet contentment. Always Christ was in control both of outer events and his own inner life.

He knew where he came from. He knew exactly why he was here and what he was to do. He knew where he was going. And this being so, nothing could shake him; nothing could deter him from doing his Father's will; nothing could diminish his desire to achieve all that he had been sent to do.

It is, of course, possible to protest that Christ could do all this because he was divine. May I point out here in all solemnity that no man, no woman, whose spirit has been entered by the Spirit of God is any less empowered. This is not to minimize the majesty or person of Christ. It is but to affirm what he himself declared, that those to whom his Father sent his Spirit would live as he did and achieve what he did.

A careful and unbiased reading of John's Gospel will make this clear. It is far better for the reader to discover such truths for himself than that I should here embark on a doctrinal discourse.

I have deliberately developed this theme on doing God's will simply because when all else is said and done it lies at the very heart of quiet, contented living. It is basically God's intended way of my taking life. It is what Jesus had in mind when he invited worn and tense people to come to him and find rest. When he told them, "Take my yoke upon you and learn of me," he was not intimating that he was going to add to their burdens and make the going still tougher. What he was saying in so many words was simply this: "I know the secret to successful, contented living. I know how to take life with its tangles and its strains and its tensions. The way I have learned to handle this load that breaks men down can be passed on to you. Just come to me and I'll teach you; I'll show you the secret."

And this secret is to do his Father's will. It is to live in harmony with his Spirit. It is to be caught up and carried along in the great surging current of God's plans and purposes (his will) that flow from eternity to eternity.

To do God's will is to become an integral part of the infinite. It is to be literally incorporated into the divine ongoings of God. It is to become more than just a partner in God's eternal enterprises, but rather to be his Son; to be a member of his family; to be one in the family fortunes of God.

Paul, with his magnificent intellect and enormous spiritual perception, saw into this sublime secret. He points out in various letters to the early churches that the great honor bestowed upon God's children is that of becoming heirs and joint heirs with Jesus Christ in sharing all of the prosperity and privileges of God himself.

This is a heady stuff for us mere mortals to assimilate. It is almost intoxicating to our spirits to contemplate it. We are told not to be drunk with wine but filled with the Spirit of God. And when the full awareness of our heritage as God's children comes home to us, it is bound to make an enormous and irrevocable impact on us.

For one thing, it is sure to shake us loose somewhat from our adherence to and reliance upon this world for either our comfort or contentment. There begins to creep over our deep inner consciousness the conviction that we really are no longer merely citizens of a country on earth, but much more, truly permanent citizens of a heavenly community. We begin to see much more clearly that we are really just passing through this earthly scene. We start to realize that all that has to do with the world is transient, temporary, and subject to deterioration or decay.

Because of all this we find our contentment, our serenity, our inner strength are no longer dependent on nor conditioned by contemporary events or materialistic values. Rather our quiet hope, confidence, and rest are centered in God and in simply identifying ourselves with him and his aims.

This is to find serenity in harmony with his Spirit, to find contentment in complying with his wishes (commands). It also adds enormous adventure to everyday living, for each day brings me nearer home.

Before leaving this thought of doing God's will and being in harmony with him, I should emphasize that this does not imply drifting through life. There is too often a tendency for us to become almost fatalistic about our faith in God and his great purposes. We are sometimes both lazy and apathetic about the whole issue. We shrug our shoulders and murmur sweet nothings—"What will be, will be."

This is not our Father's intention for us at all. We were granted free wills with the privilege of exercising them. And it is expected of us that we shall deliberately set ourselves to seek out and cooperate with God and his plans. We are to acquaint ourselves with his desires and, knowing them, we will presumably be determined in our efforts to comply with them. This cooperative enterprise between us and God becomes of primary importance in all of our thinking and acting and living. It conditions our attitudes and governs our actions. It is applied to every part of life. It has to do with everything that has been written in this book. It dominates every area of our body, mind, and spirits.

To live this way, really, is to live under God's guidance and control—not as a robot, but as an active, intelligent, cooperative member of his family. But to do this does not entail drabness or drudgery, as so many suspect. Quite the opposite. It sets one free to live in a rich and fully satisfying way. For one thing, it sets us free from always fretting over the future. The unknown is in our Father's hands, and our part is simply to do what needs to be done today with lighthearted good cheer.

For another thing, there sweeps into our spirits the over-whelming assurance that nothing happens to us by coincidence or chance. We are not the mere playthings of whimsy. We are God's children, living in cooperation with him, controlled by his wisdom and love, the objects of his unending care and deep affection.

It would not surprise me if many who read this will be extremely skeptical about it. They will question whether it is really possible for a person to live this way. To all such I say that it is. One who has learned to know and love God, who delights in cooperating with him, has come into the position of positive and purposeful living. A tremendous sense of con-tentment, well-being, and relaxation from the fret of life enfolds that person.

Now it matters not whether poverty or prosperity, sickness or health, peace or war, laughter or weeping, loneliness or pop-ularity, failure or success, make up the warp and woof of life. Behind every thread in the tapestry of our days one senses the gentle hand of our heavenly Father fashioning a pattern of unique worth and beauty.

In this calm assurance lies great peace. We are able to accept every adversity with equanimity. We are able to enjoy every tri-umph and delight with dignity. Gone from our lives are the tension, the stress, the strain of the old struggle to survive. In its place there is the gentle joy of contented living, the ability to be grateful for *every* event that comes to us as God's children. This is what Jesus referred to as living life more abundantly . . . at the highest level.

7

Help for the Higher Life

nyone who has read this far is bound to ask, if he does not already know, "Where can one get help for the kind of living outlined? Is there any source to which one can turn in order to know God better, to understand his will and how to cooperate with him?"

These are legitimate questions. And this book would not be complete without giving at least some general directions on how to know God's will and how to do it.

The first and by far the most valuable guidebook is the Bible. All through the preceding chapters, whenever I have referred to the Scriptures, I have had only the contents of the Old and New Testaments of the Bible in mind. This is a collection of sixty-six books written by some forty-odd authors over a span of history of well over 1,500 years.

I do not debate the fact that Moslems, Hindus, and Buddhists, as well as many other religions and human philosophies, have their scriptures as well. The basic difference between the Bible and other teachings is that their founders and teachers have all been mortal men, whereas the central figure of the Bible, Jesus Christ, is more than a mortal. He is the living God, active even now in our affairs. He is approachable and he reveals himself to seeking men, and reveals his Father's wishes, by his Spirit.

Beyond this I would add only one other observation. It is this, that though I have lived and traveled widely in parts of the world dominated by other religions, there was little or no evidence that their adherents had found the secret to serene living. If anything they were more burdened by their beliefs than if they had had none at all. Nor did their scriptures seem to induce any uplifting change in their personal code of conduct. For these reasons their teachings cannot be accepted as timeless truth.

It may be argued that many so-called Christians are no different. This is readily admitted. It is an accepted fact, as stated emphatically by Christ himself, that few would ever really know him, that few would find this way of lofty living. But the sincere, seeking person can meet Christ. By his teachings and through his Spirit the entire tone of life can be altered from one of tension and turmoil to one of great tranquility and nobility.

Therefore, the ultimate source of spiritual enlightenment lies in the main body of the biblical Scriptures. It requires a certain amount of time and concentration and persistent reading to grasp the full impact of what has been written there. One of the rather amazing discoveries one soon makes is that the same portion may be read again and again, each time with new delight and fresh meaning. No other material ever written has this immense depth of truth to it.

It is very important to come to the Scriptures with an open mind. There are some parts which may well prove very offensive and others which can be boring. One time will show why they have been incorporated into the collection of material. Because of this, I urge seeking hearts to begin with the New Testament and concentrate especially on the Four Gospels with their account of the life, death, resurrection, and teachings of Jesus Christ. After this move on into Acts and the Epistles. Later on one will derive great help from the Psalms, Proverbs, and the historical books of the Old Testament.

Before beginning to read the Scriptures it is beneficial to request God to enlarge one's spiritual perception of them as one reads. This he will do by his Spirit. It is the surest way to understand both what is being read and how to apply it to our lives.

Casual and routine reading of the Bible is really of very little value. We have to be in earnest with God if we are to get to know him and know what his wishes are. He is not much impressed by people who treat him rather casually with a "take it or leave it" attitude.

On the other hand, when one is extremely serious about delving into the Scriptures it is remarkable how they do indeed come alive. They become very gripping and fascinating. Their truth proves to be inexhaustible and provides enormous pleasure and satisfaction to the spirit.

As one reads, it is an excellent practice to have a notebook in which one jots down the main impressions conveyed to his heart by the Spirit of God. This is one way in which God is able to speak to us not only about himself but also about his wishes. Steadily and surely in this way there will grow upon us an increasing confidence in both God and what he says. The Scriptures will become our final terms of reference. This is a tremendously important factor in living, if for no other reason than that it eliminates much of the anxiety about what is right and what is wrong. It is not popular in our permissive society

71

to say unequivocally, "This is decent, that is disgusting." But because so few do say it, or even know how to differentiate between the two, we live in a society smothering itself in a gray fog of frustration and confusion.

Instinctively people do want to decide and know what is proper and helpful and what is not. But because most of them never bother to read the Bible they have no final terms of reference for their conduct, so that anything goes. The net result has been to create a climate of confusion and chaos in social behavior that leaves people baffled and bewildered.

It is not easy to live under this sort of strain and anxiety. It is not surprising to find young people turn in almost every direction looking for someone or something to establish a code of conduct by which they can live in confidence and dignity. In many cases they turn to the sort of creeds and philosophies which betray their better selves, and they end up feeling very cheated and even more unsure of themselves than before.

Perhaps a brief experience I had with a brilliant engineer will help convey what I mean. He was an extremely handsome man, tall, well-built, and very successful in his chosen field as a consulting forest engineer. He owned a beautiful home in a large city and was married to an attractive woman. They had several brilliant children. All of his life seemed a success. But it really wasn't. Deep down inside, this man was ill at ease and discontented with life.

He came to see me one warm summer evening. We sat out on a back patio, chatting until dark. After he had unburdened himself and told his tale of discontent, we sat quietly and said little.

Then I turned to him and said, "Really, what you are looking for in life is a final frame of reference. You are an engineer. You know that in Ottawa or Washington or London there is a bureau of standards set up. There is an exact inch, an exact foot, an exact pound, an exact measurement made for everything. So when you speak of a foot or pound or inch to another person anywhere in the world, be it New York, Hong Kong, or London, he knows precisely what you mean."

He nodded his head quietly and agreed.

"If it wasn't this way," I went on, "you engineers and the whole world would be in utter chaos. Can you imagine the terrible confusion and frustration if every engineer decided to establish his own set of standards?"

He laughed—but it was a laugh of recognition, for he already saw the point I was going to make.

"So it is with God and us. Somebody has had to set down a specific and final standard whereby we can live. He has done this for us in the Scriptures. There lie our final terms of reference. We can't possibly go wrong if we turn to the standards of the Bible and rely on them for our personal conduct."

He saw the significance of my statement. It was the turning point in his life. From then on knowing God and doing his will became to him the most important things in all the world. What is even more, frustration and misgivings soon were replaced by a deep, settled serenity in his life. Why? Because he knew he could bank on the Bible.

His personal conflicts and anxieties about his conduct were resolved. His responsibilities in rearing his family and dealing with clients were clarified. In short, he had moved from an area of uncertainty and apprehension to one of calm and quiet confidence. Now he was a man at ease with himself, at peace with his family, and relaxed in his work. This is what responding to the Word of God had done for him as an individual.

Just reading the Bible is in itself not enough. Of necessity one must comply with its instructions and cooperate in carrying out our heavenly Father's wishes. I say this is necessary simply because this is *the secret to knowing God's will.* And naturally it is essential to know God's will before one can do it. We find that as we carry out the instructions of God laid down in the Scriptures many of our more formidable difficulties are resolved.

Many people are puzzled and perplexed by what I have just said. They insist that even though they may know what God's will is, they simply do not have the ability to comply and carry it out. They assert that the standards of personal conduct set before us in Scripture are quite beyond their power to perform.

In part this is true. For so long as we stand on the sidelines, so to speak, and merely shake our heads in despair at what God asks us to do, nothing happens. On the other hand, the moment we move out of our lethargy, and in faith actually *do* what we are told to do, we discover that it is possible. This is because God, by his own Spirit, enters our spirits in response to our confidence in him and energizes us beyond our own ability. This is precisely what Paul meant when he wrote to the Philippian church, "For it is God who worketh in you both to will and to do of his good pleasure" (Phil. 2:13).

Even more encouraging is the fact that as we go on in this way we find it is not a struggle or a strain to do God's will, but a pleasure. There are too many people who consider this kind of life a sort of penance. They look on it with great misgivings. They feel sure they might be expected to do something desperately difficult. They are afraid it will deprive them of a certain degree of freedom and enjoyment.

The only answer I can give to such misgivings is something like the statement of the ancient psalmist, "Oh taste and see that the LORD is good" (Ps. 34:8). One has to try it before he can talk intelligently about it. Those who have a deep inner desire to do God's will, who are prepared to cooperate in carrying it out, soon find a freedom and joy in living they never knew before.

For many who move into this realm of loftier living there is an acute awareness that their little lives have at last been linked to the majestic and eternal purposes of God. Where before their days were but a tedious, tension-ridden existence in which they stumbled from one dilemma to another, now they sense that they are moving strongly in harmony with the infinite. There is purpose and direction to their decisions and their actions. Even the dark days and difficult times are seen not as disasters, but as disciplines that lead them to greater goals.

What is actually happening in all of this is that God our Father, by his own Spirit, is making real in us the life of the living Christ. The energy, the attitudes, the thoughts, the character of Christ are actually transmitted to our spirits and minds in such a manner that it is both possible and practical for us to live as he did. This means that even amid the most trying or tormenting circumstances of life we can live as he did in quiet strength and contented serenity.

We are bound to encounter troubles and difficulties of all sorts. We cannot hope to escape the tensions, worries, and stress of modern living. They are, as pointed out at the beginning of this book, exerting their tyranny at every turn. But we do not have to be broken and beaten by them. We can rise above them and surmount their assaults by virtue of the life and strength of God's Spirit within us.

"Greater is he that is in you, than he that is in the world," reads 1 John 4:4. And note the words of Jesus himself: "In this world you will have trouble. But be of good cheer! I have overcome the world!" (John 16:33). And so can you.

Very often people who read a book of this sort approach the end of it with a certain kind of apprehension. All along they are hoped the next paragraph or the next page might contain some special secret that would unlock all the mystery of life to them. Or they hoped for a single key to open wide the door to better living.

I cannot offer any such single solution. All that has been written in these pages is something like giving away a whole ring of keys. Each can unlock a different door to a separate area of life. It is as though I have tried to share fully all the secrets I own to all the rooms of life. Quite frankly I can say I have held back nothing. My main motivation in this work has been to try to help others to tame the tyranny of their tensions and lead them toward serenity in their daily lives.

The longer I live, the more keenly I am aware that basically all that counts in life is what we can contribute of comfort, cheer, and inspiration to others. The success of our living is measured not by what we can accumulate for ourselves, but by what we can bestow upon our fellow travelers on life's tough trail.

In my wallet I have carried a small newspaper clipping for many years. I do not have any idea who the author is, nor where it came from, but I pass on these few lines as a finale.

> To laugh often and much;
> to win the respect of intelligent people
> and the affection of children;
> to earn the appreciation of honest critics
> and endure the betrayal of false friends;
> to appreciate beauty;
> to find the best in others;
> to leave the world a bit better,
> whether by a healthy child,
> a garden patch or a redeemed social condition;
> to know even one life has breathed easier
> because you lived.
> This is to have succeeded.